I0756421

FINISHING LINE PRESS
www.finishinglinepress.com

The Birds of Poverty Ridge

poems by

Brad Buchanan

Finishing Line Press
Georgetown, Kentucky

The Birds of Poverty Ridge

ISBN 979-8-89990-404-2 First Edition

ACKNOWLEDGMENTS

"Davis 8 Unrevisited" has been previously published in *Field of Black Roses* (Wingless Dreamer, 2022)

The following poems have been previously published in *VOICES* (Cold River Press, 2023):

"A New Lease on Life"
"Garbage Day on Poverty Ridge"
"The Birds of Poverty Ridge"
"The Ghost of Poverty Ridge"
"The Porches of Poverty Ridge"

"Metempsychosis" has been previously published in *VOICES* (Cold River Press, 2024).

Publisher: Leah Huete de Maines
Editor: Christen Kincaid
Cover Art: Nora Buchanan
Author Photo: Nora Buchanan
Cover Design: Elizabeth Maines McCleavy

Order online: www.finishinglinepress.com
also available on amazon.com

Author inquiries and mail orders:
Finishing Line Press
PO Box 1626
Georgetown, Kentucky 40324
USA

Contents

I

II

III

I

From the Deserted Library Sessions

the pages turned themselves
as I waited
I knew my tender fingertips
would find those guitar strings
too thin
and painful on a borrowed fretboard
I had no other experience
to sing me through
those Tuesday lessons
all the music would come out wrong
and the money I had brought
would end as bars of chocolate
that thudding
voluptuous box on my knee
would never hum a secret dream
nor pluck at
any heart's soft sleeve
with a pick or a thumb
though I stroked its neck
no wild horse ran over its dark bridge
or waded in its awakened pond
no lyric found its resonance
in that aperture
I had nothing to say
to that smooth blond shape
as I tripped among its gracious notes
beside the shelves
full of archetypes
I barely spoke to the friendly girl
whose mother insisted
on driving me home
after a hopeful, helpless session
with a sadly accomplished musician
whose strong slim hands
seized fleeting beauty
and who taught me
that this toughened touch
was the one thing I could never learn
in that deserted library

The Grand Seaweed Dam

Too young to desire
                    or torture each other
the children worked all day together
damming the flow
                    of the creek that led
to the tourists' beach. They piled seaweed
in banks to bolster
                    driftwood logs
and mounds of sand
caressed into dikes.
                    The lank bulbs
twisted, slimy green
or desiccated
              in a mass grave,
only held for moments
                    till water
found a path to relieve the pressure.
The structure
              rebuilt
barely diverted the swelling drive
of the endless current.
I discovered it
              in ruins later
when their parents, sunburned and tired,
returned to gather chairs
                    and umbrellas
and absentmindedly called those diligent
stragglers home from
                    their joyful chores.

The Moment When

the moment when
his daughter is born
he is exhausted and alarmed
her face is waxy
clenched and pale
her ribs are heaving in and out
she struggles for breath
at the foot of the bed
he rises
tells his wife goodbye
to follow the nurse
who is rushing the baby
down to the NICU
she must survive the endless ride
in the elevator
under his bleary and wary eye
somehow
they make it through together
every day since
he becomes a father
again as he wonders
how they saved her
and what might take her away
the next time
to where he can't go anymore
he wants to watch over her
every night
as her duvet cover
rises and falls
with fear or fever
or just sleeping through
her wakeup call
like a typical teenager
on a typical Saturday morning
in a typically dreary November

The Breakfast Dishes

strawberries leave
their kisses
on the cutting board

there is marmalade
on the uneaten crusts

the past is a luxury
that we can't stomach

that no amount
of romance can rescue
although it had
a bold, fresh taste
so recently

once the zesty rinds
are swept to one side
leftover blueberries
keep their flawed shape

the brightest flesh
of delight is gone
and the rest is wasted
however sweet

The Caretaker

Collecting the precious scraps of need
that fall to me, I take good care
and leave the rest. The untouched stare
at me, insulted by my greed
for giving that lets so much go begging.

There is so little I can use
in all this human misery.

I have room in my museum
of compassion for a bruised knee,
a split lip, an irrational fear,
a pang of hunger from my 10 year-old daughter.

I treasure the miniature cry for help,
the complaints in a minor key.

My wants are modest, and so my routine
is built around feeding and clothing my children,
paying the bills and avoiding harm.

I store up the chores that afford me my powers,
and can hardly stand to be rid of them.

Dream Sequence

i

in the most terrifying dream
his daughter is calling out for help
not in despair but with confidence
that he will be there even in his absence
along with her mother
to guide her in some trivial matter
easy for a less privileged child
when he awakens, he finds her nowhere
and her cry was only his feeling
of need to be needed
and taken for granted

ii

he know he will never again
be so urgently required
as on those nights
when she had those nightmares
and he would awaken
and go down the hallway
to her darkened room
to whisper them softly and sweetly away
and thank them for being
so easily vanquished
and then linger outside
her door for a moment
to kiss the tearful monsters goodbye

My Daughter Prays

what she prays for I can't say
but I know what she prays against:
danger, death, and violence
losses of hope, removals of love
an angry teacher, a deceitful friend
I cannot see whether she kneels
but I can hear her husky voice
as she entreats the dimming day
not to take her grandmother away
not to watch her parents divorce
not to permit the Russian advance
as far as Kyiv, not to declare
the unavoidable nuclear war
not to damage her father's poor health
not to make her mother sadder
not to allow her beloved cat
to escape into the world forever
not to encourage more kids at her school
to climb on the roof and threaten to jump
not to let the virus disrupt
the long-awaited dance this Thursday
not to get sick or have anyone die
not to take her sister away
to college next summer, not to be
so lonely and scared of puberty

Where She Was From

she learns too late
that her trip is a chore
without privacy
with no time to stop
or to come up for air

she holds her breath
to stop the tears
from making noise
as the bus drives off

she realizes she never wanted
to leave home at all
let alone for so long

she dreads the absence
of delay on the tarmac
aboard the plane

she understands that
nostalgia begins
as heart-sickness
that the world is so wide
with so many strange
and desolate places

she hugs her money belt
on the train
regretting its value
and fearing its charm

she comprehends
the small size of her room
and the puny universe
of her routines

and she accepts that she
had to come
this far to imagine
where she was from

At Death's Door

at death's door
there is no barrier
or guardian
to ward off intruders
no heavy knocker
no peep hole to pose for
no posted warning
no proper procedure
no angel awaiting
no questions to answer
no formal greeting
no plan for departure
there are lights on the ceiling
and shades on the floor
but nobody watching
you have privacy
at this final threshold
you can remain a prisoner
or else go free
for no one lives nearby
except you
and you cannot enter
that other dimension
in this body
here you must leave me
and everyone
you must shed the self
that brought you so close
to being gone
that traps you now
in this in-between
your heart knocking hard
at the gates of its pain

Of the Causes of Sadness in Dying

not the letting go but the leaving
not the leaving but the missing
not the missing but the hurting
not the hurting but the knowing
not the knowing but the fearing
not the fearing but the loving
not the loving but the losing
not the losing but the forgetting
not the forgetting but the failing
not the failing but the falling
not the falling but the ending
not the ending but the regretting
not the regretting but the despairing
not the despairing but the dissolving
not the dissolving but the undoing
not the undoing but the unmooring
not the unmooring but the going
not the going but the letting go

The Pendo Dolls

They came by mail early in the new year
like sister-brides for the gods of winter;
a final present from my mother
who died a month before they arrived.

Two girls in Kenya sewed them tightly
with skillful needles and Singer machines;
Carol and Prisca made bright bold skirts
very much like the ones they wore
to cover the rag dolls' light gray skin
and wove in tiny imperfections
to render them unique.

My mother had been a volunteer
for an NGO run by a neighbor
that offered them a brighter future,
postponing marriage
with education and a business.

It even afforded some of them
traditional mud huts of their own
and a grateful independence
for a few years, before they had husbands;
after all, *pendo* means love in Swahili.

My mother gave all of herself to the world
and held nothing back,
except for this work I knew nothing about
till the brown cardboard box
turned up late last night.

I waited to open it till I was sure
that no one would witness
the sadness I saw in her sacrifice;
those sweet, soft figures were her avatars.

I wanted to learn
what message they brought
before I presented them to my daughters,
and thanked the stars
for the secrets she kept.

Distant Early Warning

he feels the lumps
beneath his jaw
and presses them
to see if they'll burst
or ooze
and simply go away
like the boil on his left side
that he lanced
when he was a boy
it yielded yellow pus
and white
like a boiled egg
the scar still fills
with skin and dust
the lumps are spreading
much too fast
to think of killing them
in the old way
and so he thinks
of telling his wife
not knowing
he is on his way
to fighting and dying
and being reborn
in ten years
he will breathe again
but in the meantime
he will suffer
and see beauty
in the disaster
lining up to pierce his lung
with a hidden tumor
that no doctor
imagined in time
the lumps recede
and he returns
to his game of soccer
and he coughs a little harder
wonders if
it might be pneumonia
lets his family
go a bit longer
thinking he will live forever

On Refusing Further Treatment

an indolent lymphoma can
kill an ambitious, vigorous man
in the prime of his life
its sickening stealth
can undermine
the health of any family
but more bitter than death
is the recognition
of the exhaustion
of human compassion
by a thousand reflexive reactions:
disbelief, dismay, disgust,
can demoralize all
but a hardened and saintly
habit of dissociation
the roughest truth is
a cure that prolongs
the suffering is almost
more cruel than failure
which, as an orphan,
can claim no relations
and make no conditions
before its surrender

On Some Nights in the Cancer Ward

on some nights in the cancer ward
the beauty is unbearable

it lies in the carefully silent treat
of the sensibly shod
                                        heart-weary relative
leaving late
                        in perfect calm
so as not to disturb a moment's quiet
on that shining floor

in the loving darkness
                                        closing in
more sweetly in the despairing room

in the merciful release of a hand
upon a shoulder
                                    to show it is time
to shut off the insistent machine

there is a ravishing
                                      absence of pain
around the corner
of the gleaming hall

from the long hoped-for
promised pill
                              that brings on
a final
            peaceful dream
in which it all fits together
at last
            and says we will end
where we began

but no one can lie
                                      under that spell
for long

its holiness hurts me
and I cry for home

While I Was Away

Tell me, did I miss anything
all those nights when I was away
living high up in the hospital's
bone marrow transplant wing?

I know of a few memorable events:
the dead bat that fell out of an air vent
right into the upstairs hallway
just outside our daughter's bedroom door,
the same one that she locked that year
so often that you had to remove
the mechanism that bolted her in
against all forms of adult persuasion;
the curious case of the special wine
my parents drank as a matter of thirst
without any second thoughts or remorse
and which your father had been saving
for some far more festive occasion;
your last-minute call to the suicide hotline
just when I was set to come home
that told you it was no emergency
to feel so desperate and alone.

Tell me again, was there anything else
while I was preoccupied with my own death?
What happened then that is still going on
behind your brave façade of health?

Davis 8 Unrevisited

I can't go back in there anymore
to the floor where I shaved off my hair
and walked the hallways
like a nightmare
gratified to find itself in caring hands
yet free to roam
and scare my ghost with a lurid reflection
where sleep was troubled
fleeting, futile
but the darkness was my own

where all harsh words
had called a truce
but to be truthful was unsafe
sick with love for endangered life
yet avid of eternal grace

companioned by a skeleton
alarmed by angels with
syringes, catheters or suppositories
I found a point of view from which
my whole life story could make sense:
a destitute, abject romance
which had the virtue of coherence

the kind of ward that killed my mother
and birthed my saddened
sweetened father

a space you can only go to recover
when you have died
to everywhere else
where every midnight is a vigil
and every morning means remorse

whose door is closed
to all the lost souls
whose fatal promise
has proven false

Herb Garden

How little space you need to plant a world.
How fragrant are the spoked rosemary quills
and the cat's-tongue-textured plumes of sage,
to name the two I recognize by smell.
I know the dense, dark weft of mint
and the tobacco-sheen of wavy basil leaves.
I sense refreshment even where I draw a blank
or turn away blindsided by the bees.
An undiscerning and unhurried visitor
less faithful than the fleet-billed hummingbird
who hovers here for nectar and to spite
our perched and plaintive quacking indoor cat,
I wonder at the maker of this mute
and imperturbable fertility,
whose absence drove me out of my cold lair
to sniff the guttered embers of a fire
to find the appetizing traces of some
spice that might have cured our wounded love.

Blood Oranges

The swollen blood oranges fall with a thump
as I rake clumsily them out of the tree.

My stilted, hooked basket can hardly catch any
when I thrust it up and jerk it back down,
and a bright, heavy rain is pounding the gravel;
soon there are bruised and cracked suns
all around.
                    I am shaking the heavens
to let this ripeness loosen and drop,
as green clouds swirling overhead threaten
yet another hailstorm of sweetness.

This, at last, is the right time to harvest
the scarlet flesh of our turbulent, succulent
rat-infested backyard orchard.

Even a man with a spiky touch
and crooked regrets in his neck and spine
may reach down to such ready refreshment.

The aromatic and beautiful damage
I gather painfully in this wild weather
is a foretaste of springtime,
an echo of summer.
                              Those that split least
will yield the juice I offer my daughters
and my wife, who will scarcely guess
how high the winds blew, or what wonderful
wreckage I've made of my life.

Death Parted Us

death parted us—
I did not die
but that soft promise
bore me away
to where you could not reach
or touch
and you too lost
what was your life
though you survived
we saw that
we had been released
from bond and vow
I broke that oath
the day I set my fatal course
seduced by sickness
to get worse
there was another
I could not forsake
in my blind eyes
the faithless light
turned torturer, adulterer
familiar demon
pale blue fire
destroyed the banns
that kept us here
revived objections
that slept for years
under all the compulsive chores
and the hubbub of desire—
a dissolving glue
we cannot renew
at a different altar
though ashes stir
when I catch sight
of you, the source
of all I loved
bereaved now twice

Irreconcilable

the parting clouds
attend our progress
suggest a faint
Utopian landscape
where strange
destinations
are unveiled
hovering
on the dim horizon
a family driving home
after a grim
vacation
just before the divorce
proceedings
the sky reminds us
that everything
could have turned out
otherwise
had we only
enjoyed ourselves
transcended the leisurely
disappointments
or convinced each other
there were better
days ahead
instead of this vista
of differences

At East Portal Park

never again
will a park mean so much
as when our children
ran its length
and stopped just short
of the limiting street
here the lost labors of parenthood
took place in a game
of pitch and catch
or a soccer practice
where nothing was learned
but everything felt
in those primitive screams
of action and consequence
where kindergarten was rehearsed
and babies released
to squirm at will
where dogs required
the jerk of a leash
as they followed the trace
of an ancient rival
all the way into a fresh new world
of excrement
where the cedar waxwings
and the crows
knit a fretwork above the meadow
and that one awful day
where the picnic was spoiled
by a mascot
who terrorized a sheltered girl
who howled to go home
before we settled in
to hear the holiday oompah band
and that green space was haunted
all the long summer
that a family just arrived
had left forever

Her Last Dance

a twelve year old with a baby face,
she was the tallest one in the troupe
that danced in the studio parking lot
in the last days of the pandemic year
a few months before Dad and Mom separate
she calls them in to watch her perform
a different dance of her own invention
to the Dance of the Sugar Plum Fairy
it is the most beautifully poignant ballet
either of them has ever seen;
they understand its futility
she is imploring a final audience
with her imploding nuclear family
the slight streak of sweat above her ears
is a measure of her desperate desire
to keep the world she knows together
if only to glimpse a distant illusion
the magic of childhood waving goodbye
with labored breathing and an off-balance curtesy
not enough to impress the gallery
(older sister and musing cat)
or fend off the looming catastrophe
after the rapturous, scattered applause
the long weekend when the truth comes out
and the future is wrenched from the past forever
and sisters shake their heads and cry
and the house is emptied of its glamor
and the too-small slippers are put away
and the glorious music is rendered moot
and the delicate fairies sour and die

A Final Contradiction

every fiber of my being
belongs here
and I am going

everyone I've known and loved
these many years
is what I'm leaving

this is no formal paradox

this is a wrenching
bitter death
upon a savage battlefield

knowing the truth
that all is lost

the proof a dagger
in my grasp
already deep
in my gasping guts

and an awful recognition

this is a fitting punishment
for every weakness
in the sinews
and the faltering of resolve

here is the ultimate
oxymoron
facing the defeated man

whose coward soul
must say goodbye
to his wife
and abandon his children

against his judgement
to meet the challenge
of a final contradiction

Towards an Erotics of Departure

I am too sexy for
my body
or any body

I desire
more embodiment
than current
circumstances permit

what I want
cannot be contained
in any skin

my drive
is negative
to the bone
and more sensuous
than you could imagine

I need the tender
invisible sinew
just beyond
the reach of my tongue

I strain for the lost
grains of a perfume
you never wore
that shares
your name

I savor the distance
that draws near you
when you imagine
that I am gone

I Forget Where We Were

I forget where we were
when we had our last perfect moment
sometime between the diagnosis
and the desperate,
                    disastrous treatment.
Was it there, in Occidental,
at the little French restaurant
so far off the beaten path
of parenthood?
                    It was just us two
marveling that the drama of cancer
staging itself inside our family
had bought us one more weekend together.

We sat outside. It was late summer.
The bread was excellent, I recall,
and the table made of fresh, yellow wood.

I had my usual fruit-forward white
and you had a muted, earthy merlot
or maybe a resinous pinot noir.
                              After that,
my memory fails me. What else we ate
remains a mystery.
                    I can still see
your warm, brave face
radiant with empathy.
                        Maybe it was all
too good to last, too sweet to be true.
Where did we go after that,
                              you and I?

II

How to Take Stock of an Empty House

i

Does one list the people no longer present?
How does one account for those who left
under constraint or with compunctions?
What is the status of a cat,
both inhabitant and haunting absence?
Who gets custody of the shared memories?
What becomes of all the false starts,
the new beginnings that didn't work out?
What to make of the traces of children,
their lives heading elsewhere, hopeful and dense?
Who will take care of all the safe places
where they hid during games that ran late?
Who will look after the dusty devices
when their lights have been switched off?
Where shall they rest their yearning glances
now that all of their loved ones have left?

ii

The bathrooms where he flushed and grieved
his bellyaches while neighbors waved
themselves goodbye
contain odds and ends of medication,
books of matches from a misadventure
undertaken with the best of intentions,
floss picks, forgotten painkillers,
hair ties, a stray toothbrush,
a paper clip, some After Bite,
combs and brushes from previous ages
a treasure trove of Ace bandages
bottles of obsolete shampoo
purchased by faulty memory
repurposed as makeshift body wash
for a happier man
than he imagines he will be again
miscellaneous feminine products
unmentionables, the tricks and trappings
of health and beauty
beyond his reckoning anyway
betokening a faithful habit of domesticity
that he has forsaken
for reasons he cannot begin to fathom.

iii

In their old bedroom he harvests an armful
of mementos to take away:
the indescribably precious gifts
of innocent creativity
an endless HAPPY FATHER'S DAY
proclaimed by a stringy signature
and superlatives accorded to dads
regardless of their true desserts
or underlying character
though he cannot claim they were truly earned
these at least he is not ashamed
to bring with him.

iv

In the basement he sits and marvels
at the trophies and medals won
playing games that now mean nothing,
at pictures from vacations gone
to populate the archetypes:
daughters clinging to the robust shapes of doting parents,
whimsical cards and school projects,
prize posters and half-finished crafts
Lego constructions that somehow
outlasted best-kept marital vows,
the rows of albums no one dares to disturb—
the feelings they hold are too fragile
to bear up under scrutiny—
the woolen blankets his mother knitted
with her full heart—before it ran scared—
folded up, sitting on the floor
they cannot bring her any nearer to him, nor to anyone
their smell is a musty comfort that threatens
to trigger his allergies yet again.

v

He damages the crinkled paper heart
as he pries it off the wall
over his disused and orderly desk
and considers whether his own will allow
the next departure, inevitable

and even somehow advisable,
since he must eat and take his pills
and watch his former life dissolve
from a safer, simpler distance
and wonders, will that broken organ
stand for another violent transplant
on this April afternoon?

vi

The living room, where he lay down
on the couch for years at a time
then got blindly up to dance
like a grasshopper at a picnic of ants,
displays a favorite wedding picture:
them, escaping in a sports car
that he was too frightened to drive for long
the one in which she looks so happy
and he so gleefully unprepared
for tragedies nobody saw coming:
the loss of his blond crop of hair
and all its sympathetic power;
the sudden, unwanted inheritance;
the lonely burden of sorrow she bore;
the wealth that ushered them to this house
then scattered them like dust in the air
to many far-flung properties
that neither of them could rightly appraise,
that lawyers will show them how to lose
if they can muster the strength to disclose.

vii

The front porch, where he gazed at the trees
with defective and wonderstruck eyes
was also the simple refuge that he
found with their younger daughter
to pause in the midst of ferocious play
or, after a very bad day at school,
to sit and watch the world go by.

viii

Here is the ill-omened ceiling vent
where the corpse of a bat fell out
like a petrified soul he surrendered one night.

ix

He labored for equity in this shared space
during the long nights in the guest room
when he soaked his sheets through three or four times
disturbing nobody with his disease;
though she twisted and burned two floors overhead,
he spared her his darkest moments of dread
and also his strange acceptance of fate
when he would depart, unsure if he'd come back.
She too earned her place in this stronghold of debts;
she paid up her share in worst fears and long hurts.
So how do they reckon with assets so deep
and such sapping expenses of tears and of sweat?
How can they calculate who should owe what,
and how shall that rough justice be brought to light?

x

In these mirrors their daughters examined
their prom dresses with joy and alarm
that yielded quiet confidence
and charmed accessories.
Her foremothers left so many treasures
for them to unearth in the secret passages
that their home's capacious frame contained,
whose wings held props to set women forth
upon the stage at which their girls gazed,
uncertain whether their right was by birth
or by such protection and privilege
as beauty seems to deserve and confer.
These were the shining pools where hair
grew into honey-colored crowns
and tapestries for their curious minds
to hang in different shapes each day
to suit the roles they chose each morning
or the performances of evening,
when everything was part of their play

and they were the authors of how they should be
looked at. Not vanity, nor in vain,
but fleeting were those moments of tense
self-scrutiny in a formal gown
or a spring-bright frock or a blouse of green velour.
She held these looking-glasses steady for them;
though much has changed,
these sliding doors stand ready to reflect
the cut and drape of their costumes back
just as faithfully; though parents had wrecked
the peaceful weather of the home,
their blooms were always there to be found.

xi

Who will inherit this priceless trove
of derelict objects, the signs of the love
they hid in plain view and can now never find?
What will become of the hallowed ground
of their stylish parties, of the parlor shows
behind glass doors where their daughters emerged
as princesses, fairies, ballerinas,
magicians, comedians, puppeteers?
Who will bear witness to the vanished hours
that burnished such beautiful built-ins and fixtures?
What doted-on child will fall next down the stairs?
Who will pass out in the darkened hallways,
half-naked, defenseless before his own mind?
What shall depart in a funeral ambulance,
poisoned by its lymphatic stream?
What lovers will cradle desires they failed?
What act will redeem where they struggled and cried?
What newlyweds nurse? What fresh dreams unfold?
What will be born where a marriage has died?

The Ring

its third and final avatar
is the one I almost
forgot in a drawer
as I was packing a last few things
from the Airbnb
where I had been staying
to move into a new rental house
where everything will have its place
except for this thick gleaming object
rounded, smooth, and cool to the thumb
a measure of all
I thought worth treasuring
ensuring me safe passage through
the throng of loveless desiring bodies
a talisman whose magic was earned
and proof against
such hurried displacement
I stash it in my rear hip pocket
like a face card I will produce
when asked to show what I have lost
in the poker game
of online dating
this, I will say,
is the one detail missing
from my profile
the one I'm still loving
with half my heart
while the other half withers
like the stump of an amputated finger
or a castoff limb
still convinced of its pain
when all its familiar connections are severed

Building a Bookcase

i

testing my osteopenia
in the construction of this casket
for the weight of decaying words
may not be the greatest idea
but why did I take all that Vitamin D
if not to arrest the insidious process
of digitized amnesia?

ii

uncovenanted, this ark contains
only one of everything
I thought it worthwhile to preserve
so nothing much will come of this
let alone a new beginning
but damn it, let's get this last screw in
before knocking off for the evening
soon I will fill these cradles full
of otherwise forgotten dreams
all twisted up in their musty sheets
like newborn corpses

iii

I've always wanted to work in a morgue
play coroner to the desiccated
litter of hundreds of printing presses
to find and analyze the cause
that brought each victim into my preserve

iv

I broke the first tall shelf I tried
to stand up against my office wall
and turned it into two square blocks
of new apartments for dusty tenants
a slumlord among librarians
I build my shoddy constructions in
the low-rent neighborhoods of my brain
where I stroll slowly, waiting for some
dim, desperate offer to draw me in

v

I am making this against the advice
of posterity, knowing nothing lasts
including the new lease I took out on life
to make it back here
where I am safe and it is quiet
I am straining to set
something permanent down
amidst the month-to-month agreements

vi

I have things to put
in their proper places
though in no particular order or pattern
and double-stacked if it comes to that
I brought them here in cardboard boxes
and paper bags that broke apart
the minute I tried to pick them back up

xii

I almost thought I might drown in them
I had run out of reasons to read anything
but wanted to swim in their inky tide
now they swamp my ankles as I wade
deeper into my ardent chore
I must sink a dock someplace on this coast
or I will never reach the shore

Fixer-Upper

of all the readymade metaphors
this one was the most overdetermined
I was a reclamation project
on those TV shows my daughters watch
"Love it or List it" comes to mind
so does "Good Bones" and "Grand Designs"
owners must be handy
or free with their money
or hoping to flip me for someone else
once I'd been smartened up a bit

I was an emotional money pit
a ramshackle wreck
whose windows were broken
or haunted and streaked
whose soul had sunk
through its cracked foundation
that seemed like it ought
to be razed to the studs
or dug up for something new
to pour out a nice modest brownstone
or craftsman-style home
for a wistful widow
whose children were gone or going soon
but I shook and refused to tumble down

I've shifted the ground on which I stand
but I'm still that eyesore across the road
from our first house
where the half-homeless died
and fucked and played that horrible music
until two fires condemned the place
but not before I had moved away

I am somewhere between a permanent loss
and no fixed address
hoping for a new owner
nevertheless

Where the Heart Is

home was once where
my heart belonged
I had no wish to yearn beyond
the topless tower of my room
whose walls protected many dreams
of gentle animals and their schemes
of statecraft or of sportsmanlike
vainglorious battles
where no one got hurt
now home is where
my hardening heart
may rest for a moment
on its journey out of my body
into the lengthening lives of my children
forward into the care of a woman
I first met barely two weeks ago
it is an unforeseen succession
of rented spaces
and creature discomforts
where I balance precariously
between nostalgia for lost love
and the endless possibilities
of wearing my desire on my sleeve
and seeing who plucks
on the dangling thread
that may yet unravel my whole future out
through the labyrinth
where I have always resided
though I tried to imagine it differently
never knowing what I wanted
until it was too late to inhabit
and always afraid of what I protected:
the simple secret of being present

His Old Neighborhood

his old neighborhood
was always expensive
costly to get in
and to get out of
took him for everything he wasn't
thought he had what he really didn't
dragged him along
to some well-heeled parties
turned on him when he couldn't afford
his wife the easy pleasures they shared
held him at arm's length
an interloper
a foreign object
a carpetbagger
not the sort of person who stays
in a bad marriage
and cheats where he can
at a club or at cribbage
an awkward stranger
who somehow mismanaged
his job and his health
and who ends up expelled
to the farthest edge
of the right part of town
they call Poverty Ridge
where the restaurants date back
a generation
or are links in a chain
binding up his digestion
but where rent is affordable
and he feels free
to park where he pleases
there's no cheaper way
than this to exist
yet he often returns
to the streets
where his daughters
still feel more at home
where he wrote the bad checks
that his friends never cashed
where he mortgaged his heart
defaulted on dreams
found himself paying tax
on a hope slowly dashed

Home Improvement

I dreamt that we tore out the janky staircase
and built a new second floor to code
that we extended the back deck
and put in a heated swimming pool
that we built new raised beds for our plants
and herbs and flowers, then gave our daughters
their long-awaited separate rooms
replaced the old rat-infested garage
with a guest house and an office
with beveled windows overhead
chased away the atrocious neighbor
who drank and set his house on fire
and I woke up with a mouth full of praise
for our endeavors, those shared adventures
in home improvement, in being parents
who had provided that optimized structure
I was proud of what we had created
because we had done it all together
then I realized the credit was yours
because I didn't live there anymore

Sorting the Photos

These tokens of our ambiguous loss
have found their way into my custody
as duplicates of the ones you kept,
the surplus of former felicity.

The girls appear smaller, more innocent,
their poses a sop to posterity:
in the thick of the fray with budding cousins
or standing aloof in a ceremony.

There are snapshots of me dressed up and dancing
at a party where I didn't want to be;
of my parents, enraptured by a present
conferred on their anniversary.

There's a jarring image—from a vacation
I dodged like a bullet, ungratefully—
a lock upon a fence inscribed
with our initials: you plus me.

I see first days of school with ironical smiles;
hysterical yawps for a holiday;
precarious postures with pumpkins and knives;
impossibly dimpled dexterity.

I cannot choose which ones I should keep
or tell how I could stand to throw any away,
but here I am, stubbornly sorting the photos,
shuffling ghosts in their bright array.

More vivid than when I experienced them
as blurry shades in my damaged eyes,
more fugitive in this thinly sliced form
than playing cards, they fall astray

from my numb fingers, slip through my hands
like time itself when you and I
loved so much we made children to frame
in the glossy illusions of memory.

The Buried House

An old man growing sick and weak,
I want a place to live as I like
after my death, so I order the earth
hollowed out, and a house built beneath
the level ground. I enter it, chuckling
at my own cleverness, look around, checking
to make sure all of my wartime trophies—
the human skulls, the peace entreaties—
are there, awaiting interment with me.
Satisfied, I close the door
and give the signal. Workmen pour
loose dirt and rocks, seal the windows
and stop the entrances. Darkness piles up
all around me, praise is heaped
upon my roof. The distant slap
of spades dies out. Finally alone
with my ancestors, I grope, sit down,
and wait for the air to grow dense and full,
as my whole life was before this illness.
If my last ambition falls short
and the spirits fail to rise and invite me
to rule their kingdom, one comfort remains:
no living eyes shall see tears in mine.

A Day Without Daughters

a family seeing a family off
with separate sighs of regret and relief
that such a visit need not be prolonged
that such a community can't be sustained
reminds me of my freedom today

a day without daughters is a recipe
for the lonely contemplation of trees
and the murmurous rumination of leaves

sorely lacking a human function
I drift out my windows in search of direction
pause to collect a fallen pattern
and press it into a book like wisdom
some ways of being no longer make sense
some forms of life now stand aloof

I have lost my place in the tiresome dance
of parenthood, and I grin with grief
that the pretty pictures taken today
at the rustic cottage will not feature me
nor will my absence signal alarm

no tedious explanation shall form
in my co-parent's brain; we have somehow earned
enough apartness that no one is harmed
when I stay away, awake and at home
wishing my darlings a slow, safe return

Those Small Hours

the camp to which
my daughters were sent
sadly at first
for kids with cancer
in their families
offered them joy
within a week
renewed its magic
every summer
made them homesick
nauseated
at the different
difficult food
empowered them
somehow
to speak of disease
in their own words
out of my hearing
and it helped them
to grow wise
in ways I can only
begin to imagine
on those late nights
around a fire
talking of death
and gratitude
in those small hours
they were safe
among strangers
learned from others'
hard news
and bitter truths
accepted
temporary relief
from big problems
and helplessness
tasted their tears
and found them sweet

A Truly Sick Man

a truly sick man is not lonely
he has disease for company
a silent friend to make him angry
or a bewildering enemy

he courts fresh treatments in the hope
of earning a reproachful slap
or side effects to pinch and grope
he swoons in the doctor's loving grip

the back of his hand knows its strong veins
are fit to use by any means
no needle or stent in them will burn
his blood will flow till no patient remains

he waits in the keeping of medical students
influenced by he knows not what enchantment
his mask gives back a stranger's exhaustion
or the insolent roar of a revving engine

today he might need both of his canes—
the white one and the pseudo-blackthorn—
which he has kept out of loyal affection
but might deploy in self-protection

a chorus from the parking garage
sifts into his ears, so plaintively soft
that he straggles blindly, honking his grief
until it gives him a new way to laugh

a sick man has no use for the truth
he only wants what will bring him death
or a pleasant and convenient berth
on a spaceship bound for a second Earth

Near Miss

nothing else
would have mattered
had I consummated
that encounter
on the freeway
merging slowly
under the late
afternoon's averted
foggy lunar eye
she and her Toyota Echo
were in the blind spot
I thought technology
had abolished
so soon after
a reckless driver
had swerved between us
what was she doing
in my unconscious wish
for a convenient death
so painstakingly avoided?
I want to thank her
for her welcome alarm
for the prompt
self-righteous honk
of her horn
so many hard times
would have been
for nothing
had her reflex
not intervened
I try to recreate her face
from memory
long hair and glasses
a woman's harsh
expression of protest
at my shoulder
a vengeful fury
out of a nightmare
offering me
this gift of shame

Painless

painless, I'm on another planet
a vanishing world at spectacular twilight
where injustice, corruption and violence
and filed away under "current events
that will always be with us,"
according to the pet eschatologist
of this imperious hemisphere

I'm unknown to the latest emperor
in his sagging Armani suit
and the pylons that bestride the highway
are beacons of hazardous disrepair
to which I am sweetly indifferent
at the wheel of a hybrid metaphor
that is not the vehicle of my death
though my inattention abuses its power

all eloquence is just a deathbed speech
a lavish soliloquy of desire
approaching its ultimate exclamation

a peace so restful always proves fatal
its beauty lies in the gentle twist
at the tail of a narrative
that has rung too loud
and for far too long

suicide is no name for this crime
this is the omission of any grave aim
or deeper purpose
this is the relief that finally does justice
to so much pointless suffering

this is *sub specie aeternitatis*
seen through the windshield
still buckled in

In Good Spirits

amidst the bad news, there is this
affecting nugget: against all expectations
I am in good spirits

which might mean almost anything:

I have an extensive collection of booze
with the odd pretentious bottle
hanging around for a desperate interval
when I shall have no time to sweeten
the assassins of pain
but need their intervention
lest my swinging moods start to worsen
for once and for all

I have a wry smile that masks a terrible
guilty pleasure in mere survival

I tell dirty jokes to subvert my shame
at the predicaments I am avoiding
dealing with in public at least

I have a dark secret that I am concealing
with all my powers of friendly dissembling

I am being very brave
in the face of another disease
by crying every time I'm alone
by writing my next last living will

I have decided upon the means
by which I will seek an ending
to all repressed feelings and quoted emotions

I have left behind all the muted groans
that made my lost life so worthwhile

A Band-Aid Solution

from now on
this is all that I want:
a strip of thin latex
over the skin
they punctured
and pounded
and ripped away
the flesh wound
is shallow enough
to become
a simple discoloration
with time
a wine-stain
a birthmark
a badge on the bone
a band-aid solution
to the aching within
is the perfect
course of treatment
from this day
the cure is worse
than the disease
paper over my cracks
so that I can write
a proper account
of the slow demise
I will neither defer
nor accelerate
leave all the rifts
to widen beneath
the tissue of lies
I will gladly endorse
for appearance's sake
let the rot fester
keep a straight face
the broken tip
of the spear
went so deep
I can only postpone
I can never escape

Biking Drunk

downtown
I biked like
I had zero fucks
to give or even
to throw away

I blundered in front of
a clanging train
scandalized
another two lanes
of onrushing traffic
that swung past
unseen
till too late

I might well
have been struck
and killed
or at least been
dragged
through the streets
by my backpack
on my crashed
and burning side

instead I veered
through
a blinkering haze
that jeering
blaring maze
of self-summoned
menace
and motorized outrage

what was I thinking
as I lumbered unsteadily
from that instant
of monstrosity?

damn
I should have died
they let me
get away

Desiderata

my final nurse's reassurance
that it's okay to let go
a last confession
from my conscience
of the things I could not do
a downward glance to reconfirm
a soft landing
for my trust fall
a good excuse for refusing further
responsibilities as a father
a loving smile
from a healthy daughter
a voicemail greeting
for the hereafter
pre-recorded on my phone
a gentle executor's fatal hand
to mark the archive
of my soul
a meal
politely to refuse
or gnaw on nervously at the close
of my tormented embodiment
a pill to chew on
to speed the thrill of dissolution
a gag for my earsplitting
agonized howl
a bucket for
the indigestible
remnants of my exploding skull
a blanket to bite on
a towel to besmirch
with a farewell speech
from an orifice
suddenly out
of my modesty's reach
a sweet illusion
to undo the curses
of resentment and remorse
a moistened washcloth
for my face
the certainty
of a resting place

Touchstone

beneath the brittle
ossified skin
my fingers find it
giving way under
this tender pressure
a rooted button
that triggers nothing
it has the false profundity
of a suicidal fantasy
palpating it
is like jumping off
a vertiginous cliff
only to find
the water is warm
and not quite
shallow enough
to fulfill
my final request
it must be gone
by sunset tomorrow
a useless port line
is a time bomb
reaching through
the jugular vein
and into the heart
it sits
like a modest medal
hard-won
and harder still to jettison
the frozen pole of
my melting being
the still, grave center
of unseen healing
the buried truth of
my shameful persistence
the last secret
of my precious
suffering
a bloody treasure
that needs forgetting

Closing the Portal

when they pull out
these tentacles
the plastic squid
with the fleshy bulbed head
the port line through which
many nightmares seeped
that will only
gradually dissipate
they'll leave a vacuum
with a whorled scab
at its exit door
a sutured tube
folded over itself
a second umbilicus
hacked off
and sealed
closed to further inspection
an oddly darkened
window annealed
into perfect opacity
a pinned medal
ripped away to reveal
no more than an itch
to the sensitive touch
a grave colophon
to the tortuous story
of my brittle
bewildered body
and its perdurable
purblind disease
an aspiring scar
for a silent lover
to look at in wonder
if not to admire
a rabbit hole filled up
with moss and soil
a gate slammed shut
to the underworld

Hole

the hole in my chest
has a vacuum tube
stuck into it

they are drawing this out
as with forceps
a white-hot filament

prolonging
the agonized expression
of nothingness
through ingenious means

such pressure to heal
amounts to discomfort

the prosthetic is
yet another headache

the minefield
they have left behind
is a void I must negotiate
on tender hooks
of burning flesh
with thinning
and dissolving skin

this is the fulcrum
of my new life
and I must wince
in addressing it
with even a trace
of self-compassion

this is the steep hurdle
over which
my unruly sleep
must be ridden

this is the latest
shallow grave
from which I have
not yet arisen

Disconsolate

my dead mother takes me on a tour
of winter landscapes
I sob and sob inconsolably
she wants to show me how the air
can frame each little white falling star

all I want to talk about
is how much I loved my vanished in-laws
and the house I built of sand
in which I tried so hard to live
as it slowly fell apart—
I dug deep, gathered soft wet handfuls
to fatten the plaster
but nothing held

she shows me why I had to escape
before the roof caved in on my head
I risked live burial to atone
for the many days
when I walked with the dead
without her guidance

she leads me up a precarious path—
there's an avalanche on either side—
I stumble, shiver, and cannot follow
her implacable example
nor her mute and loving lesson

the beauty here is chaotic, frozen
and full of unspeakable remorse
the meaning here is not the earth's
nor mine to interpret

I find myself safe and in her absence
she has only come to haunt me once
since she passed into purgatory
beyond my control or my compassion

she wants me to feel her implicit judgement
her final forgiveness
her heartbreaking silence
one last time to show me the vanity
of all those helpless good intentions

III

The View from 2217

i

a gap in the trees
just above the roofline
affords me a tiny
fragment of highway
where cars and trucks
pass in opposition
like the most distant
revolving rings
on a saturnine planet
of which I am
the only human inhabitant

ii

farther in lies
the Heavyside layer
where dogs walk
their owners
and American crows
and dark-eyed juncoes
are heard
and a white-crowned sparrow
cries over them all

iii

closest to me
is the canopy
of bushes where
the beaten wings
of a little nuthatch
sound an alarm
amid green buds
and purple bulbs

iv

this is my new universe
sitting so still
that unseen footsteps
clapping downhill

stir the deep pool
of contemplation

v

two tail-lights burn
like embers of coal
and a conversation
leans into silence
the purr of a motor
accumulates
stretches
and disperses
like a pack of feral cats

vi

the colors drain
towards the sunset
drawn by a strange
gravitational pull
that infects
my itching eyelids
with an exhausting
crepuscule

A Last Byzantium

The lesser goldfinch
and cedar waxwing serenade him
and his younger daughter.

She tells him about the first ten amendments
that comprise the Bill of Rights
and wonders at the uselessness
of the second and the third.

He tells her about his favorites:
the first and the fifth
which he can appreciate, as a poet
who talks about things
maybe more than he should.

He wants freedom with impunity
just like the birds in these evergreen trees.

This house is his earthly paradise,
the rented reward for a lifetime of searching
tirelessly for himself
in the twittering, dizzying towers
of stilted speech.

The music of words has followed him this far
and abides his final questions:
is it worthwhile to hammer out
a manifesto on his deathbed?

Can the much-maligned scarab
roll yet another ball of dung
into something magisterial
if not exactly palatable?

He will not be forced to quarter
the drunken louts still bearing arms
in this self-destructive colony,
and that is one reason to be grateful
amid the torpid anarchy.

There descends an unnatural calm
when the passing sparrows have let
their last cries fall on ignorant ears

and he requires a device to reveal
his own lost thoughts to himself.

In the long hour just before midnight
he wants a myth to intercede
and save him from yet another spell
of incomplete unconsciousness,
a tantalizing dream of metaphoric identity.

Instead, he makes the blind trip to sit
for hours, agonized, on a toilet;
a tight fist dug deep into his gut
praying for the right parts to ooze out
and not the last vital organ (his heart)
or else to hear one more morning chirp
from a western bluebird, a finch, or a lark.

A mourning dove, he can hardly believe
his ears, has reached him again with her broody,
muted cooing. The laws of nature
are winning him over at long last
to his self-consoling, consuming task:
the writing of a new constitution
to come to terms with the rites due the dead,
the dying, and those who will die someday.

His is a desperate anthem for everyday
symptoms, the poignancy of a country
still too young to imagine its history
from an eternal point of view
which, he admits, is too far away
for him to summon anyhow.

Only the ephemeral earns
his serious attention today
and his daughter has long since gone inside;
the winged seraphim have returned to the sky
and it is already a cooler evening
than he can endure for very much longer.

He sings you goodbye and he signs his name
in the guest book of God
where nobody will see.

The Birds of Poverty Ridge

this is the domain of the barn owl
and the yellow-rumped warbler
and the house finch
and the rock pigeon
among other avian avatars—
all my local rivals in song

the bushtit
and the California scrub jay
accompany me on my errand today
a quest to find out where we all are
somewhere west of Newton Booth
an enclave of mission-style architecture

a Nuttal's woodpecker
offers a love tap or two to assess
the sturdiness of arboreal structure
and craftsman design
a northern flicker deserves its name
on its flitting way to someplace else
in concert with a graylag goose

a red-winged blackbird
comes to crown
my search with its
satanic thorn

citizens of this humble rise
on a flat-as-piss-on-a-platter maze
of grids and trees
we are at least not poor in noise
and do not lack variety
of tweets and thrums
the poetry of neglected feathers
and gawping young

these are the cries
of my neighborhood
in all its beauty
and disrepute

The Crossing

the man with close-cropped
peroxide hair
and a shopping bag hung
from the crook of his arm
has just crossed
four lanes of highway
that have stopped
to let him pass
and hopped the concrete barrier
into the barren no-man's-land
that marks a dormant
construction site
intent on his own divergent journey
as the crow flies
and yet hemmed in
determined to complete his errand
he is no ordinary
pedestrian
he is a voyager on a journey
with no path
no warning sign
no entry point
no exit strategy
he is convinced
that a different thoroughfare
must be followed
stubbornly
he cuts against the grain of traffic
forces progress to a halt
on a mission
of his own conception
towards a goal that cannot wait
for any recognized intersection
nor seek guidance
from any light
outside his innermost
guiding star
invisible at this rush hour
with four more lanes to negotiate
he has signaled his desire
to brave each stranger
in each car
and carry his luminous head as far
as possible in the dimming air

The Invalid of Poverty Ridge

he moved in a few months
before we met
he was noted for his recalcitrance
on cleanup days in the neighborhood
his rapid succession of second-hand cars
the eternal vigil of his television
his way of dispensing Gatorade
to the homeless teenagers
the sudden, lewd bang
of his janky screen door
his raging addiction to feral cats
his fussiness in parking at
just the right distance from the curb
his cocksure manner
of falling down steps
his affectation of various canes
his ill-assorted selection of hats
his invariable rotation of sneakers
and jeans and sunglasses
his paper-thin skin under too many clothes
he was always so overdressed
in speech and most of all in summer
when he was said to disappear
for weeks at a time
in that unfinished basement
where he was eventually found
that same year

The Paradoxes of Poverty Ridge

Here the homeless escaped the flood
that levees failed to withstand;
here rich families drove them out
when the valleys drained.

Here I won a bitter freedom
costing everything;
here I lost that trailing phantom
who wanted me for his own.

Here the gardener comes on Fridays
to fill up the bin;
here the backyard bursts with sweetness
that the rats consume.

Here I gather strength for a journey
stubbornly postponed;
here I shelter from the daily
devastating sun.

Here the wide world seems far worse
than I had cause to fear;
here I come to terms with death
and deem it premature.

Metempsychosis

we all traverse strange states of the soul
on the long transmigration
we must undergo
have moods like catastrophes
that soon reveal
themselves as defeatist
delusional
or neurodiverse to the point of genius
or shattering self-destructiveness
but some have a sixth
or a seventh sense
to guide them through their inward haunts
a passing acquaintance
may show us a map
a portal to spaces where all our worlds stop
as if before a bed where a child
suffers insensibly
fevered or chilled
and our chair is a pew
and the doctor an altar
at which we fling prayers
that bind us forever
although a first death
comes in handy sometimes
when we've lost our way
in the labyrinthine
galaxy of possibilities
where our lives form
a four-dimensional maze
that we run through somehow
with a single thread trailing us
a personal god
who dogs and divides us
from what we have been
and forces disjunctions
between dreams that come
in rapid succession
like linear time spliced into infinity
frame by warped frame
and we spin on the axis of all we have done
and end in the same moment where we began
retrieving each memory for good or ill
denying, assenting
reliving it all

The Ghost of Poverty Ridge

one foggy morning he gets up and goes
to the house where he lives
to give his cat her medicine
then he proceeds to visit his children
to watch them open
the presents he gave them
he cannot see a hundred yards
ahead of him, nor can he retrace
the steps on the path
that led him into this festive limbo
this in-between bliss
and this ignorance is all he knows
he haunts the places
where he must accomplish
his daily tasks and rise to the spirit
of the holidays when
like agonizing clockwork, they come
he lends them his eyes but not his heart
it is too late to mend his ways
or render them harmless
his sins amount to not very much
he has committed to nothing since
he was a child
when all he loved was a small gray mouse
who encompassed his world
and brought it up short
of what most adults would call a life
he has never existed
outside the confines of his brain
and its infinite, innocent
ceremonies of self-possession
now he must wander
in search of belongings
that have no relation
to where he has been
absent and searching for all this time
at home on this interstitial plane
of want without need
of lack without loss
of guilt without crime
never knowing the cost of anything
but the value of all
he has missed

Et in Arcadia Ego

the skeleton in a Santa hat
prolongs a horrific holiday
beyond any haunting salutation
to serve a salutary function

death too exists in the giving season
and even those without skin or hair
can benefit from some spurious cheer

have vanity enough to conceal
a white pate from the chilling air

can even be prevailed upon
to chortle in a sepulchral tone

reassure the fat that the very lean
have festive spirit in every bone
and would at least enjoy the taste
of the rich air escaping a winter feast

what shall this untimely vision inspire
in everyone who sees it there
perched on a ground floor balcony
performing inertia as irony?

I nod and smile at my famous old friend
whose secrets I will keep safe with my own

Garbage Day on Poverty Ridge

biking the gauntlet of fallen palm fronds
and the piles of thorny debris
and the plastic slalom course
of recycling and yard waste
and the thunderous underpasses
reeking of cancerous poverty
climbing the littered, deserted sidewalks
chasing the waning rays of the sun
I am somehow getting home
though my address is something different
than insurance or the government know

the warthog tusks of a foraging cop car—
props of a masochistic desire
to know all evils and summon all sins—
turn slowly away
they are letting me go one more time
for some reason
though I may menace pedestrians
stalled before bus stops
or gazing lovingly at their phones
in private thrall to a publicized medium
that cannot imagine anything
let alone the immediate future

the season is turning
the trash is collecting
the whole city stinks
and the last light will fall
and rise and stagger
and fall once again
and I am straining
at the least resistance
these streets can offer

I'm retracing a path
through this labyrinth
to arrive at where I began
only too happy
to sniff at the ass-crack
of yet another
breathtaking dawn

The Porches of Poverty Ridge

the many objects on our front porches
are no-one's idea of riches
go unnoticed there for years
unprotected by fence or grate
a few yards from the freeway on-ramp
our priceless crafts find the weather harmless
they include little pots of flowers,
a colorful abandoned toy,
ceramic planters, basketballs,
gourds, apotropaic elves,
playhouses, empty bird cages,
fire-red lanterns, Ukrainian flags,
pails with assorted gardening tools,
unlit candles, wicker tables,
weather-beaten lawn furniture,
immovable classical urns full of dirt,
barbecues with no chains or coverings,
watering cans from the last millennium,
Adirondack chairs in miniature,
folk art collections curated by children,
bundled rugs for the next donation,
an ashtray with its unmatched lighter,
a mailbox jammed with unwanted paper
a seasonal declaration, a string
of lights protesting the gloom of winter,
a gift in limbo, a stroller awaiting
another adventure, a sprinkling
of leaves from the darkening sky,
a welcome mat, a drying blanket,
a cardboard box containing nothing
or something priceless gone astray,
someone's as yet unprocessed recycling,
a love seat that has seen happier days,
free bottled water for thirsty travelers,
cement blocks, rockeries, bricks, and brooms,
a package to take in or take away
monitored by a cyclops eye,
belongings outcast and disclaimed
or liminal creatures frozen and filmed,
temptations for a passing stranger
or offerings to a wandering neighbor
the *lares* and *penates* on
our daily altars of the unknown

The Thunderstorms on Poverty Ridge

i

the water in my basement flows
and pools and drains as the rain falls
I putter, glazed and apprehensive
looking for other spots of blockage
where sump pumps fail to prevent or manage
the daylong downpour into foundations
and their cherished spacious assumptions
is my home the ark of some covenant
with the god of tenuous tenants?
or does my entire neighborhood float
on a premise of near-catastrophe
that carries off the weaker inhabitants?

ii

in this tense dry interval
I set out on a wary patrol
assessing trees for their looming damage
and power lines for their height of voltage
the sky is the color of watery milk
behind a cracked glass, tinted dark
and the calm on the streets
feels a pulse of alarm
that clangs in the lights
of an oncoming train
the grating rakes sweep and the city trucks trawl
and dredge debris that the last week has hurled
untended into the thoroughfares
knowing this is a momentary reprieve
a merciful echo of the silence
that will descend for good or bad
on the besieged streets of Kharkiv
the corpses we gather are few in number
the disaster is of a gradual nature
a slow mutation of climate change
through the cycles of drought
that make the rains
especially destructive this year
not the iron whim of a dictator

iii

I mop and squeeze and sweep and purge
myself of subterranean thoughts
make much of my newly adopted cat
and watch my freshly restored TV
for a hint that all this will be far less serious
than it seemed from the first reports
relish the shelter that still stands
around my lamely lubricious bones
and warm myself from within with a drink
from a bottle for which I have Costco to thank
calculate the hours of life
left in my devices so lately charged
sweep up from the wasteful holidays
postpone my once-imminent demise
for yet another leftover year
indulge in some overdue home repair

iv

the violent wind is a nightmarish presence
a poltergeist in the bones of this house
that rattles the windows and shakes the doors
and strains the frames of my bedroom and stairs
a crazy chime sounds a bell of alarm
and my children cower in the beds above mine
the power is cut to ribbons
with a swirl and a whistle
and I am frightened to move a muscle
or to lie prone in one place for too long
every fiber of living wood
and dead fixed beam is tested again
and against this force and itself
so great a tension must give out
and topple trees or break roofs apart
or send loose wires through brittle glass
and ragged shards into innocent hearts
eventually but somewhere else
my craven prayer amounts to this

vi

my neighbor scrapes and fusses with twigs
barks orders at me until I snap
and so the smallness of human life
dissolves the sacred mystery
of resilience and tragedy
though a giant lies in agony
uprooted, prostrate before our eyes
the morning after the blue oak fell
the gawkers proclaim it a miracle
that nobody was killed after all

Morning on Poverty Ridge

a wealth of sunlight
shows the day
its preciousness
my lavish bruise
has faded into
a deep vermilion
the dining room is steeply lit
and the living room shines
from within and without
the shadows fall
into many shapes
around each framed
and simple object
the beauty of my decadence
is realized in this
ideal stillness
the limited energy
in my body
resonates with all this static
symmetrical space

it is not yct noon
but the height of peace
has been attained
after many months
of trouble and strife
my elusive mind
escapes
to contemplate
the loss of life
a world away
where the dawn brings only
the renewal
of an old hostility
here the same bright beams
show abortive infancy
the aftermath
of bullets and bombs
atrocious deaths
a mutual enmity
where both sides
are plunged into
darkness already

Stick Man

if religion is another's crutch
then this stick of faux pagan yew
is my heavy-handed excuse for a switch
from invalid to intrepid pedestrian
along with my Moroccan hat
justified by my alien origin
and unforeseeable destination
it insists on taking me out
for a late afternoon stroll in the sun
now that my father and daughters have gone
I must invest myself again
in the habits of a solitary man
perform my daily constitutional
with the dignity befitting my station
on the slow pilgrimage to martyrdom;
a veteran, say, genteel but lame
speaking inscrutably into his phone
his fingers visible through the worn
tips of his gloves; a broken man
pacing gamely towards his doom;
an ancient inmate on death row
who has exhausted his final appeal;
a noble rogue wounded in a duel
who winces at passing pretty girls;
a crippled wizard; a defrocked priest;
a middle-aged man with a chronic illness
who would rather try to charm the world
than lament, disappear, or scold—
whose measured walk is a form of art
enhanced by a weapon that shows he is hurt
until he stops and hears a snatch
of birdsong, opens his hand to lift
his palm up high to catch its name
between the gusts that the soft leaves sift
and offers his cane as a place to perch
for some sweet fugitive well out of reach

A Phenomenology of the Song Sparrow

this is not
an ornithological journal
but a journey through
the preconditions
of latter-day lyricism
the diary of an author returned
from death at the hands
of post-structuralism
determined to sing
before a fresh case
of bird flu lays him low again
he just wants some words
to accompany him
on his trip to the store
some ragged lines
to help him evade
the rush of traffic
and the onset of trains
not wings to fly invisibly
beyond the reach
of time and space
but a way to walk through
a particular place
like one of its last inhabitants
recording its changes
of light and shade
for one to whom all this
will be denied
forever someday
to show people lived here
with light green hair
who snatched at stray whiffs
of marijuana
and staggered half-naked
and barked their terror
in a country called California

Colloquy of the Finches

the house finch
and the American gold
conduct a voluble
dialogue
upon the doctrine
of holy nests
and the divine prophecy
of trees
they praise their own
stewardship of insects
warn against
the sinful bees
enunciate their springtime
appetites
in punctilious liturgies
respect the far-off
cardinal
but worship only
in their local presbyteries
this canopy of cloudy skies
is their parish
and their paradise
and when they die
their wings belong
to the peasant worms
they prey upon
no wonder that their song is loud
and uncontested
no disputations
or heretics harm
their homespun
theological teachings
nor do their tweets
offend or shame
they are keepers of the sacred
ecumenical
and ecological
hifalutin and humble dream
that all our migrations
are manifestations
of God's unchanging love
on this earth
of our bones

Phoenix

The ashes from which I must rise
are only last night's sweat-soaked bedclothes;
they stick to my skin like soft stigmata.

I drag my nightmares from my bed
like a shivering bride a discarded veil
in the middle of her wedding night,
naked but for what she most wants to shed.

The fire they cling to burns me yet—
a sciatic nerve that rages on
long past the consummation of bedtime,
fed by embers that kindled my blood
and brought the roof beams down on my head.

The farthest thing from a soaring bird,
I will fall and bruise myself again
raise purple marks on my pallid flanks;
this fragility is my last secret,
the hidden truth of my royal past.

Now I search the world for forgiveness,
my tangled wings between my legs,
astonished that in my quest to die
I have failed yet another test.

Proprietary

the mossy spot
to the left of my porch
where the homeless man
camped out
that first year
of the pandemic
is sheltered by
a camellia tree
and its splotches
of red blossom
have lain like rose petals
all this winter
I wonder if one night
I overhear
two young lovers
employing this bower
I might not just
overlook
their trespass
and be the custodian
of their desire

Getaway

encouraged by my guidance system
I pursue my professed intention
to escape through the rain to the coast

not the least of my concerns,
the weather relaxes, lays down its arms
and I drive under the gray battlements
on the horizon in search of more storms
born of emotions or desires

suddenly, out of powder-blue skies
there comes a downpour—
more than I wanted, less than I asked for
which also ceases, all at once

the amphitheater of such events
is full of suspended expectation
I enter the numinous coliseum
in a gladiator's armor
a charioteer with a single charger
under my stirrups
a surge of power in my spurs

I am outpacing my expectations
and limitations
I am trafficking in fear
and fearlessness

I am trusting my need
to make a confession long denied
and once again entrusting my fate
to cement, then gravel, then dirt
recognized through
these changeable skies
by a satellite overhead
as free from mudslides and fallen trees

through tossing winds and nudging floods
still-passable highways and surface roads
incline to me, and power grids
run alongside like cheering kids
and then freeze into scarecrow poses
the onrushing afternoon goes by

in a succession of twisting vistas
and slow tableaux
that rotate and roll themselves away
while my purpose holds its velocity

a jerk at my tail shuts the gate of my thrall
and discomposes my reverie
I'm compelled to complete
my fragmented thought
by tapping my brakes aggressively

the spaces between these words must be
long enough for safety but not
so great that I drift off or stray

the turnoff comes at just the right time

I need a fresh page for this story of mine
to find its own shape and its own momentum
though the passing of trucks
will buffet and frighten
with the violence of their forgetting

the journey eases me into a verdant
panorama of sunlit slopes
and I remember what I have come for:
the soft swale in the small of her back
her silent composure's gentle collapse

The Sea Ranch Chapel

a specimen of Californian
mystical naïveté
shaped like the shell
of a sea snail
the non-denominational chapel
rests on a cradle of boulders

tiny lizards
slither through
the hundreds of cracks
which spiral out to form a path
for all visitors

the wood and stained glass door
is never locked

inside there are mosaics and pews
a metal sculpture
something both celestial
and submarine
dangles from a vaulted ceiling

the craftsmanship is impeccable
and peculiar to a Pacific vision
of collective
inward contemplation

a place of stillness in the forest
saved from fire
by the moisture of ocean air
kept from the violence of the surf
by a half-mile of hilly terrain

a sanctuary for the random guests
who passing choose
not to pass by
but to stop and wonder
at their own respect
for this unattended masterpiece

Driving North on Highway 1

the sinuous road on this craggy coast
defies the brain of cruise control
so I must tame it with my foot, unspool
its gently twisting hills
and brake at hairpin
intervals
it's sunny, but the ocean is full
of rippling clouds
the road unfurls a future of carefully chosen words
and screeching commas
I push, then pause
until the unseen yields to views
of steepest greens
and darkest blues
between which I must trace
a path
with the soft pulsations of my breath
through breathlessness
round a ledge of cliffs
where bathos beckons like
senseless death
and landslides threaten
on narrow roads
in the vertigo of truth that guards
each verbal aerie
my diction climbs this promontory
and syntax slips round each bend of the mind
to seek a symbol on safer ground
for on this highway I alone
am responsible for what I learn and what I forget
here fate is not an accident
but a swerving mistress
whom I court
with grave evasions and a furtive heart
that takes dictation from a chauffeur
who knows too well
where we both are
just past Fort Ross on Highway One
making good time through burned-out land
respecting those coming the
opposite way
set on our own course
inexorably

What Will Survive of Us is Love

(after Philip Larkin)

inside each long-term survivor resides
a devotee of the commonplace
an aficionado
of nothing special
an amateur in everything

those in whom love
is so strong
can suffer almost anything
they break fevers and not vice versa
they are the ones
who sometimes live
to a hundred and thirteen

their gratitude
is for the chance to give
yet more of themselves

they could go on forever
if circumstances would permit
such a passionate defiance of fate

they could nurture a million pets
a thousand children
and never give up

the secret to eternal youth
must be to have your heart
broken to bits

then painfully to reassemble it
over and over
only to present it again
to someone else

yes
the old wives' tale is true
what everyone should know
they do

Crow Rescue

a black wreckage of wings
on the sizzling sidewalk
hopped sideways
struggled into flight
at my approach, but you
got close enough to touch
the stumbling feathers
and crazy beak
you seized it gently
boxed it up
so it could be kept
in the back of your car
you showed that courage
is not absence of fright
but recognition
of a greater imperative—
a helpless creature
needed succor—
meanwhile the neighbor's
little daughter
watched in anguish
and in awe
as your strong hands carried
that sky-dropped burden

she wished that she
might be as brave
and full of grace
when she grows up
and a scary thing falls

Envoi

not gone
nor forgotten
but farther away
a girl at a different
and better school
is on the path to
womanhood
in some unspoken
mysterious sense
and it is all right
to cry about that
because it is
beautiful
and she deserves
to fulfill the promise
of quieter days
with a new degree
of appreciation
for all her new friends
and the next
expectations
she will exceed
even our predictions
and come to be
all of what she is
destined to dream
and to learn
she will always
be welcomed
back home when
she needs
a little less freedom
for a few days
or as long
as she doesn't mind
folding her wings
to fit through
the small door
from which she
has escaped
into limitless air

Song of the Black Phoebe

granted
it is desperately sad
to seek solace in a new neighborhood
where nobody knows me from Adam
where so far bad neighbors
outnumber the good
my text to my daughters
has gone unacknowledged
I know I occupy Nisenan land
unceded and bone-rich
my own transformation
is guilty and strangely incomplete
perhaps a black Phoebe
is just the bird
to lift my congested
dispirited head
its song is a little diminuendo
a note pair going from high to low
a triggered alarm with a trail of sorrow
telling me I will never
can never belong
but my own backyard
is as magical
as any other property stolen
and all humans look roughly the same
from its heaven
of grasses and moss
of beetles and caterpillars and wasps
my life is as good
as the next man's
and worth just as little
to the natural cycles
through which this bird
has chosen a mate
or pecked out its share
of a ripening fruit
for centuries beyond any ancestor
I claim to know
who might alter my future
or make me forget
I am time-struck
suspended
renewed
with each trill

Brad Buchanan taught British and Postcolonial Literature, as well as Creative Writing, at Sacramento State University until his retirement in 2016. His writings have appeared in more than 200 journals, and he has published four book-length collections of poetry, among them *The Scars, Aligned: A Cancer Narrative* (Finishing Line Press, 2019) and *Chimera* (Finishing Line Press, 2022). He has also published three academic books, a medical memoir, and a novel: *Spy's Mate*.

He was diagnosed with T-cell lymphoma in February 2015, and underwent a stem cell transplant in 2016. He is currently Northern California chapter leader of Man Up to Cancer, a support group for men coping with cancer. He also facilitates recurring online Writing As Healing workshops through the UC Davis Cancer Center, Cancer Bridges, and NMBTlink.

www.ingramcontent.com/pod-product-compliance
Lightning Source LLC
LaVergne TN
LVHW090534110826
845146LV00003B/1091

9798899904042